SHINGLE STREET

SHINGLE STREET

Blake Morrison

Chatto & Windus
LONDON

Published by Chatto & Windus

6 8 10 9 7 5

First published in Great Britain in 2015 by
Chatto & Windus
Random House, 20 Vauxhall Bridge Road,
London SW1V 2SA
www.randomhouse.co.uk

Addresses for companies within The Random House Group Limited
can be found at: www.randomhouse.co.uk/offices.htm

The Random House Group Limited Reg. No. 954009

A CIP catalogue record for this book
is available from the British Library

ISBN 9780701188771

Typeset in 11pt Minion by Palimpsest Book Production Ltd, Falkirk, Stirlingshire
Printed and bound in Great Britain by Clays Ltd, St Ives plc

Penguin Random House is committed to a sustainable future for
our business, our readers and our planet. This book is made from
Forest Stewardship Council® certified paper.

Printed and bound in Great Britain by Clays Ltd, St Ives plc

For Kathy
and in memory of Karl

'This year also, on the festival of St Martin, the sea-flood sprung up to such a height, and did so much harm, as no man remembered that it ever did before. And this was the first day of the new moon.'

— *Anglo-Saxon Chronicle*

'A more desolate region can scarce be conceived, and yet it is not without beauty. In summer, the thrift mantles the marches with shot satin, passing through all gradations of tint from maiden's blush to lily white. Thereafter a purple glow steals over the waste, as the sea lavender bursts into flower, and simultaneously every creek and pool is royally fringed with sea aster.'

— s. baring-gould, *Mehalah: A Story of the Salt Marshes*

Contents

SHINGLE STREET

The Ballad of Shingle Street

'If a clod be washed away by the sea, Europe is the less...'
— JOHN DONNE, *Devotions*, 'Meditation XVII'

On Shingle Street
The summer's sweet,
The stones are flat,
The pebbles neat
And there's less rip
When tides are neap.
It's fine to swim, or fine to try
But when the sea runs fast and high
And skies turn black and cormorants weep
Best watch your step on Shingle Street.

On Shingle Street
The shelving's steep
With stones to skim
As if they'd feet
To hop and skip
Across the deep,
To pitter-pat and aquaplane,
Again again again again,
Not flip and flop, and splash and drop,
The opened trap, the hangman's rope,
The cairns that mark where life gave out,
The muddy dark off Shingle Street.

From Shingle Street
To Bawdsey Bay
The sea-mews shriek
Above the spray,

The rolling seals
Are charcoal grey
As though burnt out or singed by grief.
Like ash-streaked mourners, half-possessed,
They duck and bob and stare to land
In hope that we might understand.
But nothing helps, we fail the test,
They hang and gaze without relief
Beyond the reach of Shingle Street.

For Shingle Street's a single street,
A row of shacks in stone and wood,
The sea out front, the marsh out back,
Just one road in and one road out,
With no way north except the spit,
And no way south except on foot,
A cul-de-sac, a dead-end track,
A sandbanked strand to sink a fleet,
A bay, a bar, a strip, a trap,
A wrecking ground, that's Shingle Street.

On Shingle Street
As sunset seeps
Across the marsh
The flocks of kale
Are grazing sheep,
A soft pink light
Sneaks up the beach
As if each stone were ringed with fire,
As if each pebble stored the heat
Of past disasters, past defeats.
And in the dusk they tell a tale
Of burning boats and blistered flesh,

And you can't help but watch and hear
And smell the oil and taste the fear
And feel your skin scorch in the heat:
You won't sleep sound on Shingle Street.

On Shingle Street
The stones are neat
And warm as stoves
Beneath your feet
Like aga-lids
That store the heat.
But just an inch or two below
It's sloppy-wet and cold as snow.
The lips are dry but not the mouth.
The tide's come in though it's still out,
The icy north's migrated south.
The oven tops are just a cheat.
Beware the tricks of Shingle Street.

For Shingle Street's a sneaky street,
That smiles and mangles, lures and wrecks,
Where water strips and winds dissect,
Where sea-kale bows its green-grey head
As waves wash up the new-made dead,
A bolt-hole built with ghost-white stones,
A charnel house for ancient bones,
A beach, a bitch, a crypt, a con,
A bight, a morgue, a scam, a tomb,
A sun-trap strand, a catacomb,
An angel with a nasty streak,
A seabird with a razor beak,
A double bluff, that's Shingle Street.

From Shingle Street
To Orford Ness
The waves maraud,
The winds oppress,
The earth can't help
But acquiesce
For this is east, and east means loss,
A lessening shore, receding ground,
Three feet gone last year, four feet this,
Where land runs out and nothing's sound.
Nothing lasts long on Shingle Street.

On Shingle Street
The grind goes on,
A churning bowl
Of sand and stone,
A watery mix that unbuilds homes,
Unearthing earth, unlaying land,
Tall waves that flash like silver spades,
And bulldozed buffs and quarried bays,
Not give-and-take but take-and-keep,
Just shingle left on Shingle Street.

For Shingle Street's a sinking street,
The worn-out coast's in slow retreat
With lopped-off bluffs and crumbling cliffs,
And empty air where churches stood,
And houses perched, and fields and woods,
And no known means to stop the rot.
A breakers' yard of rusted hulls,
Where combers come and herring gulls,
A holding bay for washed-up trash,

A rest home for the obsolete,
A hole, a heap, a wreck, a wrack,
A nomad's land, that's Shingle Street.

On Shingle Street
The sea repeats
Its tired old tricks,
Its one-man show,
The drumrolled waves along the strand,
The bass-line thud and cymbal-clash
As stones are stoned and pebbles dashed.
Again again again again
The waves collapse, the flints resound,
The tide runs in and takes the ground,
The tide runs out, the ground slips back.
Variety is not the name
But that's the point – the sea's the same,
Unchanging grey, the one sure thing,
A flooded plain in plain disguise,
A level field that hides its rise
Through constant ebb and constant flow,
Unlike the earth, which shifts and shrinks,
Unlike ourselves, who have to go.

Flotsam

I remember it like yesterday:
the bell buoy tolling in the rivermouth
and the bodies laid out on the beach.

Their faces flickered in the torchlight
and the buttons on their uniforms
glowed like fire tongs by the hearth.

*

Fire. Or maybe just samphire.
Burning petrol. Or a storm petrel.
Flames in the marsh. A setting sun.

*

Sib-sib, went the bird. *Sib-sib*.
'Is that a dunnock?'
I asked the twitcher as he passed,
'A siskin, a bunting, a chiff-chaff?'
He was dressed in green
like a man of the woods
and roped with long-range lenses.
Sib-sib, went the bird again. *Sib-sib*.
'There,' I said, 'listen,' and he did,
his ear tilted like a satellite dish,
but he couldn't tell me,
or wouldn't tell me,
and stepped away towards the hide
with a curt 'G'day'.

I raised my binocs
in hopes of a glimpse –
wing, tail, anything.
But the bird stayed hid
and its call faded
behind the reeds and the radio masts.
Sib-sib, sib-sib, sib-sib.

*

There's a hiss in the reeds, a shush in the surf.
Scrunch your heel in the sand and it whispers.
There's a secret, you know there's a secret.
But the shingle keeps it. The pebbles stay schtum.

*

The sea's all frills.
It flounces in
with a roll of eyes
and lift of underthings,
riding your way
on a roar of applause
till the flashbulbs go off
and it slows and stops,
turning back
with a lacy hem.

*

The wind-shaven bushes on the cliff edge
peer through the sea-fret like sentries
while daggered prows sneak up the beach.

The maltings, the saltings, the sandlings, the stone.
The fishmonger with scales on his arms.
The mirror-light of mudflats at dawn.

*

One year when we came down
a line of shells had been laid
from the water up to the shacks.

Not just shells but bones,
feathers, cuttlefish, claws,
anything bleached by the sea.

White as lime or cremation ash,
the line ran straight as a die
through flocks of seakale and pea.

The ghost road, we called it,
as though the dead had crawled
from the sea and left this trail

across the shingle to the reed-beds,
where at night if you listen hard
you can hear them plotting revenge.

*

The starfish on the foreshore.
The starling in the saltmarsh.
The starlight on the sea.

The firewood in the hearth-grate.
The fireflies in the reed-bed.
The firestorm in the surf.

*

The sandpipers run ahead
like thoughts we've not yet had,
their legs whirring like watch-cogs.

*

tideswell seaslap crabscrawl
windscut landslack sandsail

*

Slim ditches through the reeds,
a herd of Jerseys by the sluice,
and beyond, where the marsh gives out,
a combine with its dust cloud of wheat.

*

Campion, garlic, pea and kale,
and a scrubby goat willow in the marshes
and a stunted apple tree in the dunes.

*

How the river fretting in the marshes
would love to meet up with the sea.
But it sulks in scummy pools,

under the thumb of a shingle bank,
while the waves live it up, just yards away.

*

White sand, white bone, the skull of a catfish
and an oystercatcher's skeleton,
the wind through them like a piccolo.

Evacuation

June 1940. Just a dozen of us
living there. Then orders came to leave.
They sent a lorry. Back and forth it drove
all day, heaped with packing crates and mattresses.
We lived on the end so they came to us last,
the light dying as I swung myself up
and squeezed into a gap behind the cab.
As we rattled up the lane to the sluice,
a cardboard box of best china in my lap,
my heart was a nightjar churring with sadness
and hope.
                At the bend by the bridge our clothes horse
fell out. I didn't shout for the driver to stop.

Covehithe

The tides go in and out
but the cliffs are stuck in reverse:
back across the fields they creep,
to the graves of Covehithe church.

From church to beach
was once a hike.
Today it's just a stroll.
Soon it'll be a stone's throw.

And that path we took
along the cliffs has itself been taken,
by winter storms.
The wheat's living on the edge.

What's to be done?
I blame the dead
in their grassy mounds,
the sailors and fishermen

longing to be back at sea
who since they can't get up
and stride down to the beach
entice the sea to come to them.

Dunwich

The sea's a flat grey slab,
like a flattened gravestone.
John Brinkley Easey

had a slab to himself once
in the woods behind the cliff,
his epitaph facing inland

so passers-by, like us,
who'd walked up from the beach
would read his name and dates

and wonder how he'd drowned:
by swimming too far out
or as one of the crew

of a fishing boat lost at sea?
We never did find out
and later the waves took him back,

his slab disappearing in a cliff-fall,
like the graves in the churchyard,
like the church itself.

Sea Walk

When we come in March
the cliffs have backed away,
abashed by the ocean's passion.

The clay can't withstand
the constant harassment.
The trees look scared to death.

Carissimo

Remember the year the sandbank appeared?
We swam out through breakers for fifty yards
then fetched up on a yellow colony,
and marched about as if we owned the place,
two giants on an unmapped island,
the waves like excited natives
clamouring round our feet.

On the way back a tethered speedboat was rocking.
We slithered up the side of it and in,
and lay among ropes and life jackets,
the sun on my back as I tasted salt,
and you whispering something,
the same few syllables over again
like water swishing through the hull.

I thought it was 'trespassers'.

Wet

While stars swam round
in the blackened sea
and night-flowers bloomed
I lay in wait for him.
And I was wet for him.

On the Beach

We lay in a hollow on the shingle,
while the sea bowed and scraped below.
The stones were warm until I slipped
my fingers in and felt the wetness.
For a second I saw a seagull
flying high inside your eye.

When you sat up afterwards
a row of pebbles stuck to your back
like medals awarded for bravery.

Wedding

Next time let's do it on the beach,
not Sri Lanka or St Lucia
but Shingle Street

with the reeds for organ pipes,
the cormorants as ushers
and shell shards for confetti.

Your veil will be sea-spray,
and once the gulls have heard our vows
we'll exchange amber rings

then walk the bare stone aisle
to our wedding bed:
no flowers, no photographs,

only the first cold touch
as we slip from our clothes,
then happiness forever after

or – that other word for it – oblivion.

The Discipline of Dogs

In the café on Dunwich beach
I saw a woman buy a 99
and give her spaniel first lick,
its tongue neatly curling to detach
the twirly flourish at the tip
and resisting even a nibble
of the serrated chocolate flake
poking sideways from the middle.

Her trust rewarded, she then tucked in,
and beseechingly though the pooch
stared and slavered from her lap
the woman wouldn't let up
till every last mouthful was gone,
even the blond hollow butt-end of cone.

Anglers

The anglers come with rods and spools
and cast for haddock, skate and cod.
They squat beneath green parasols
like holy men possessed by God.

They fish all weathers, day and night.
Their bait is lugworm, crab and squid.
They live on tea and luncheon meat.
They have no time for wives or kids.

But they are patient with the sea
which gives them more than friendship could
or work or booze or priests or books.

The twitching reel, the flashing hook,
the keepnet stashed with silver goods,
the music of eternity.

Wave

Remember the dream you had, in the chalet on top of the dunes –
how you woke on the sofa bed to find the sea against the window,
as though you were staring at a tank in an aquarium. You knew the water
would rise and overwhelm you, but what you felt wasn't fear but anger:
no one had seen this coming; the early warning system must have failed.
Then you were back before it began, down on the beach, reading the signs.

Nothing obvious, just a pencil line at first, a scrawl on the horizon,

like arrested low cloud or a stubborn fog bank,
till you notice it's bigger than it was ten seconds since,

not a mountain but a range of foothills spanning the skyline,
a range you might speed across the desert to, by jeep,
but you've not moved, it's the foothills that are heading to you

and though they're far off you think you can hear something,
less a rumble than rising white noise, the hiss of a windsurfer
cutting through wake or the skitter of a dinghy with the wind at its back –
nothing clamorous, you could be lying on the beach and not notice

and people *are* lying on the beach, deep in a book or fast asleep,
it's only the paddlers in the shallows who've noticed something odd,
the tide drawing back, beating a retreat, *reculer pour mieux sauter*,
but the bathers don't speak French and though you've seen tidal waves
in picture books the thing now coming towards you looks different,

flatter and more insidious, with a bulge like the bulge in a spinnaker,
and what's worrying isn't the height but the weight, the miles of ocean
at its back, for whereas most waves have a curl to their lip, as if just playing

or being ironic, there's a swell and gravity to this one, a seriousness that says
it means business, not like a wave that breaks enormously then withdraws,
exhausted from the effort, no, this wave will keep going, regardless –

two plates in the earth's crust set it off some while back,
the pair of them overlapping like the shells of mating turtles,
or maybe a landslide caused it, or volcanic eruption, or nuclear bomb,
whatever the cause, no dam or barrier can withstand the fallout,
and the sunbathers who've finally noticed can't hotfoot it to higher ground,
there are miles of marshland and coastal plain before the first hill,
and no roof's tall enough to save them, or you, it's too late for that,

because the waterwall is here, the sea-cliff, wave-mound, ocean-bore, surf-glut,
carrying fish and fishermen and all manner of wooden spars and snap-offs
from canoes, clippers, cutters, coracles, catamarans (every craft a hovercraft
when the wave first hit, but then pushed under in the crush and pummelled
to pieces), so that hulls, beams, oars and paddles are coming your way
and even if they miss and you're not done for right off by a keel
ramming your skull or a mizzen mast crushing your ribs, the sheer force
will shove you down and you can forget those fancies you had of staying safe

inside the wave's clenched fist, the one miraculous survivor
(like a surfer crouching on his board under arched green roofspace),
because the horizon's overtaking you and the sea with all its debris
sweeping you up and next thing you're inland half a mile among bulrushes
like a sleeping infant gently rocked and creeled in its reed basket,
kittiwakes flying heedless overhead while moorhens thread the marsh
through which search parties will later have to wade, the Red Cross worker
with the mask over her face stooping to retrieve a tangled grey sheet,
then retching to find a body, *your* body, though for you that's immaterial.

Yes, this is the dream you had in the chalet, the one that keeps coming back,
whatever the weather, whichever the sea, even here, far from the Pacific,
on a summer's day, by the east coast, where small breakers stroke the shingle
with a sigh and shush, the wind barely stirring, herring gulls quietly bobbing
like buoys. 'Restful' you'd write if this were a church with a visitors' book,
except you read it as the calm before a storm
                                        or imagine the sea
will keep on coming as it did in '53, though wouldn't wipeout in an instant
be better than this slow deletion, as the sea rises and the cliffs are beaten back,

and you receding in step, your bones thinning, your hair whitening,
and the thing that will kill you already triggered and on the move

but taking pains to stay hidden inside you like a flood tide hidden in the sea.

Caution all prose hogs.
Poetry's a speed bump.
It's there to make you slow down.

Bonus

'Time was when poetic talent came dearer than gold...'
– OVID, Amores, 3.8

This poem is my annual bonus... I know, I know,
most folk slog away for a modest return with no extras,
and *their* work's in the public interest,
teaching and healing and cleaning and stuff. Whereas...

But I'm a poet, and who are you to interfere
if the powers above choose to reward me?
Remember the value of the words I generate
and all I contribute to the cultural economy.

Be warned: if you deprive us poets of our bonuses,
we'll be forced to move and work abroad
in a different language, and London will lose its place
as the poetry hub of the western world.

Is that what you want? No? I thought not.
You're just jealous of the cats that get the cream.
Go on, admit it: we're worth our bonuses.
Every stanza. Every line-break. Every half-rhyme.

Hacking

This poem has been hacked into.
It was meant to be a private conversation,
the line made secure with end-stops.
But someone cracked the code and listened in.

I hate to think how it will be read
when all I talked about in confidence –
the pizza, the piazza, the back row of the Plaza –
is out there in the open, on the page.

It's not my fault the text went viral
but I feel I've betrayed your trust.
What kind of world are we living in
when poems become public property?

In future I'll keep my texts oblique
so that no one can decrypt them
or discover what I'm driving at
when I speak of the ibis in the rain.

Then my hotline to you will be restored
and you can love me again, as you should:
whoever you are, whatever your name is,
these words are intended just for you.

Prism

This poem is a surveillance device.
It is checking your emails, intercepting your calls,
reading your thoughts before you have them.

When that secret you'd not tell to a soul
bobbed past us like a Coke can in the river,
we hoicked it out and stowed it in our files.

All citizens need protecting from themselves.
We've made copies of your intimate photos.
We know the websites you go to for your kicks.

Remember those words you wrote in your cups?
That you thought you'd erased? We found them
in the ether, awaiting transfer to a dropbox:

The empty bird-feeders sway in the wind.
There's light through the mesh where the nuts were stored
and the seeds for the goldfinch have all flown.

Seminar

'...if a Sparrow come before my Window, I take part in
its existence and pick about the gravel'
  — JOHN KEATS, letter to Benjamin Bailey, 1817

This poem is you, sitting in a seminar.
You would like to join in but know nothing about
zones of contestation, problematised binaries,
performativity, generative rupturing
or the ideology of transgressive epistemes.

Luckily others in the seminar do know,
or talk as if they do, or anyway talk.
So you can join the starlings on the telegraph wire,
ride that pushchair with the sleeping toddler,
hide in the blouse of the woman at the bus stop.

Just make sure to be awake, before the end –
nod, applaud, rap your knuckles on the table,
as if you've been enlightened and inspired
and when you leave the room will see the world afresh,
no longer baffled by its hermeneutics.

'It Was Good While It Lasted'

This poem is Jimmy Savile's gravestone.
Or was. Given the risk of public outrage
and as a gesture of sympathy to his victims,
it has been removed from the page.

Nor will the exhumation of his body
from the concrete-encased gold coffin
in which it lies at a 45-degree angle facing the sea
be documented in this quatrain.

Whereof we cannot speak except
with prurience, sanctimony or inspired
retrospective wisdom,
thereof we must not say a word.

Redacted

'The raw material was a substantial document... It was initially so heavily redacted by the MOD that it was almost impossible to understand'
– MARGARET EVISON, *Death of a Soldier: A Mother's Story*

This poem has been redacted
in the interests of national security.
It's an inquest into the death of a serving officer
heard at a Coroner's Court for the MOD.

On May 9th 20██, Lieutenant ███, who had begun
his first posting, at Fort ███, just twelve days earlier,
undertook a routine patrol with members of his platoon,
including two guardsmen and an interpreter.

It was the aftermath of the poppy harvest
and their instructions were to dominate the ███ area of Helmand
by repelling Taliban insurgents
and winning local hearts and minds.

Five minutes after leaving base they came under fire
and took cover in a compound, behind a high mud wall,
where Lieutenant ███ tried to radio for reinforcements,
briefly standing in the entrance doorway to get a signal –

which was when the bullet hit, finding the gap
between his body armour and his collar bone
and knocking him flat on the sandy ground.
'Man down!' his colleagues shouted. 'Man down!'

Guardsman ▮▮▮ radioed for a helicopter
while Guardsman ▮▮▮, the team medic, wiped the blood
from the hole in his right shoulder (the size of a 50p coin),
staunching the flow with a field dressing as best he could.

Still under fire, Lieutenant ▮▮▮ was placed on a stretcher
and carried through irrigation ditches back to base; the ride
was bumpy but he kept talking as he lay there
and even asked for (and was given) a cigarette.

While waiting for the arrival of the helicopter team
he was injected with morphine in his right thigh
and a HemCon bandage applied to the wound.
But his pulse was slowing – the bullet had ruptured an artery.

The Blackhawk helicopter arrived forty minutes later.
During the flight Lieutenant ▮▮▮ suffered a cardiac arrest
and, though operated on in hospital at Camp ▮▮▮,
he failed to recover consciousness.

Further tests at ▮▮▮ Hospital in the UK, following his transfer
by plane, confirmed the absence of brain activity.
Parents and friends spent time at his bedside,
before the life-support machine was turned off next day.

This poem's sympathies are with his family for their loss,
but it is satisfied that everything possible was done
to save the life of Lieutenant ▮▮▮
and it therefore refutes any suggestion

that his body armour offered scant protection,
that his Bowman radio did not work properly,

that the medical equipment supplied to the troops was inadequate,
and that the sixty-five-minute delay

between the bullet hitting and the helicopter landing –
the product of a communication failure or of
a navigation error on the part of the pilot –
was what cost Lieutenant ██ his life.

Nor can this poem judge whether his deployment
as platoon commander on his first tour of duty
in an area notorious for insurgents and snipers
was negligent to the point of criminality.

As to claims that the war in Afghanistan is unwinnable,
that young soldiers are being used as cannon fodder and that
their deaths serve no purpose whatsoever –
to comment would be inappropriate.

In short, after hearing all the evidence,
the poem concludes that Lieutenant ██ suffered injuries
that were regrettable but unsurvivable
while on active service for his country,

his death being the result of 1a) necrosis of the brain
due to 1b) major blood loss due to 1c)
a gunshot wound. Signed, ██ ██, Coroner,
acting independently for the MOD.

Inappropriate

This poem is having after-hours drinks.
What a nice dress you're wearing. Is it silk?
No need to slap me – I was only checking the material
you're made of. Shall we carry on talking upstairs?
Suit yourself. I thought you were a girl with ambitions.

This poem is texting pix of sex with its ex.
What's the issue? She's a celeb these days
and celebs love to put themselves about.
You can see what a slut she was. Revenge?
I owe her nothing since she dumped me.

This poem met a sweet young thing backstage.
How young? It didn't ask. You don't, do you,
or didn't then, and she seemed sophisticated,
sucking cock. We're going back fifteen years.
She'd be twenty-eight now, by my reckoning.

Lent

This poem is for Lent – uncluttered
as a freshly cleared draining board,
no one talking and no food on the table,
just the cut-off stalk-ends of a daffodil.

Exit Interview

This poem is my exit interview.
I'm giving HR my reasons for leaving.
They sit there, like psychiatrists, taking notes.

I was happy to begin with, I tell them.
No new arrival could have asked for more:
kindly mentors to help me find my feet,

sleepy afternoons in the sunlit atrium,
a screen and keyboard to disseminate my work.
Records will show that I made good progress,

hit it off with colleagues and line managers
and met the targets I was paid to meet.
What's changed then? No gripe about money or status,

just a feeling I've accomplished all I can.
Oh, I know where I'm off to isn't rated,
that no good word has ever been said of it.

But think of the perks. No stress, no deadlines,
no gossip by the water-cooler, no sick building syndrome,
no team-building awaydays, no commuter gridlock,

no morning glare, no dusk shadow, nothing at all
for ever and ever – an unbeatable package
I tell them, closing the door behind me as I go.

Rape

Rape, rape, you cried, nothing but rape:
flashing fields of it off the motorway,
the colour of American school buses
or the highlighter glowing on my desk.

That yellow's too violent, Miss Hartley said,
as I mixed my palette in primary school,
or was it you who said it that morning
on our way to the wedding near Diss?

Rapa, rappi, brassica napus:
once it ran steam engines,
now it's biofuel and cattlefeed
or the oil served in bistros with your bread.

Each year the country gets more Day-Glo,
the acrid lemons and noisy ambers
overwhelming the watercolour hush.
Rape, rape, you cried, with weeping eyes.

Deer

In the lee of dusk
when no one's round to see
the shy brown deer
file from the wood
and cross the field
to crop the wheat
that had reached five feet
but was lopped last week
to leave just stalk
and scrats of grain
which is what they eat –
their mouths in the earth
but their eyes like glass
tipped up to catch the light –
till dogs at the farm
on long steel chains
catch a whiff in the wind
of their sweat and heat
and set off such a storm
of yaps and barks
that the air turns dark
and the snap of a twig
makes the deer take fright
and they race as one
back to the wood
where their brown patched coats
and grey salt rumps
are lost to light
and they slip to the source
where there is no one.

Cottage Down a Lane

Remember the cottage with the pointy roof,
the one we cycled past, near the lane end,
opposite the bluebell wood, all on its own,
with missing tiles and rotting window sills,
and hogweed and brambles over the door?
The witch's house we christened it,

If ever it comes on the market, we said,
but next thing the grass had been strimmed,
the windows and soffits freshly painted,
a climbing frame and swing appeared
and a year-old Audi parked by the gate.
We never saw a soul when we passed by

but soon the toys grew into mountain bikes,
and then one evening every light was on
and music thrummed so loud
that ears were trembling in the wheatfield
while an upstairs curtain streamed across the sill
like a genie escaping from its bottle.

Remember? If you do, you'll want to know
that I drove past the other day and noticed
missing tiles and rotting window sills,
and hogweed and brambles over the door.
But bluebells shone like nightlights
and a muntjac was rustling in the wood.

Happiness

'...but the occasional episode in a general drama of pain'
 — THOMAS HARDY

Cloudless skies, old roses coming into flower,
a breeze flicking through *The Mayor of Casterbridge.*

Toasted granary bread with damson jam,
a pair of goldfinches on the bird-feeder.

The whiff of fennel and rosemary,
the farmer's quad bike leaving the field.

Two deckchairs in the shade of a weeping birch.
Everyone you love still alive, last time you heard.

Passing Places

Scotland was meant to be a holiday,
a place to escape my family –
to wander, take ferries and camp.
Salmon farms, highland cattle,
lambs like schoolgirls in black-and-white socks,
oystercatchers patrolling a loch:

I felt restored, taken out of myself.
But the roads were single track, with passing places,
and every few miles, however remote,
there'd be a graveyard, neatly walled off,
so that my stops for a piss or coffee
landed me among my namesakes,

Daniel, Duncan, Megan, Margaret
and a host of other Morrisons
whose passings from earth were written
on stones half-hidden by moss and lichen.
The words said nothing of their lives
but sometimes the dates said it,

'aged 5', 'aged 10', 'aged 17',
the rain flooding their chests,
the snow clogging their lungs,
and the futures awaiting them –
nurse, farmer, architect, mother –
swept away like a branch in burn.

As I climbed back in the car
I counted the blessings of my time –

phones, antibiotics, central heating –
though no technology masters death
and no mason will redeem me
with epitaphs as lovely as theirs:

'The finger of God touched them and they slept.'

Heather

The heather threaded through the radiator grille
was proof we'd been to the Highlands,
and the canvas on the roof-rack that we'd camped.

What else can I say? That it rained all week,
that the windbreak blew over on the shingle,
that the saucepan on the Primus failed to boil.

Home seemed as far away as Africa.
The yellow pills I took to stop me feeling carsick
were the first thing I threw up.

Grey lochs. Black glens. The sepia troutbeck
where the horsefly stung me. Ferns too tall
to see over and mist too thick to see through.

In the photos I seem to be enjoying myself.
So it's strange how I remember hating it
and even stranger how I long to have it back.

The Road to Wales

'Life is first boredom, then fear.
Whether or not you use it, it goes.'
    – PHILIP LARKIN, 'Dockery and Son'

'You're old before you know it then – poof! – over, end of life.'
Dusk, the low sun blinding us, my dad at the wheel. Next week is
my tenth birthday and here we are, going off together for the first
time. He flips down the sun visor. It's been all boredom
till now, a slow journey from Yorkshire to Wales. Then
the traffic clears and he puts his foot down. 'Death's nothing to fear,'
he says, overtaking a cattle-truck, 'it comes to us all.' Whether
they're meant to or not, his words fall like a shadow and I can't move or
speak. Of course I know everyone dies, but till now I've not
considered myself among them. 'Welsh border soon – do you
know what the time is?' he says, changing up a gear, 'I could use
a pint.' At the pub he buys me half a shandy and I sip it
slowly, savouring the bitter new taste. 'We'll be there before you know it,'
he says, turning the key in the blackness of the car park. 'Here goes.'

Learning to Swim

You stood waist-deep, cupping my chin,
while my legs kicked up a storm behind me.
Paddle those arms! you'd shout, taking a step
deeper in, as if I'd got the hang at last
and, if I dared, could swim right past you –
till the moment came for you to let go
and I'd be under, in chlorine or brine.

A woman once took my face in her hands
to test the weight of my love,
but no one since you has held me by the chin,
and though I swim as well as the next man now
I've not succeeded in getting past you.
Here I am, years later, still in your hands.

Old Men Sighing

I never understood it,
how in the places he most loved –
the car, say, or at the dinner table –
my father would stop talking and sigh,
and so long and low and sorrowfully,
like a dredger on a boating lake
bringing up sludge and weed.
Was it his death he was seeing?
Couldn't he guess how that made
the rest of us feel? Didn't he care?

Now like him I've started sighing
for no reason. *Just that time when...
if only I'd...* all the haunting almosts
and the one implacable was.

The Dressing Gown

Twenty years on, your dressing gown
hangs from the bedroom door
waiting to come back into fashion.

Short, thin, with mauve and blue stripes,
it was more for the beach
than round the house,

a thing you'd drop in a heap
as you ran into the sea
then towel yourself dry with afterwards,

stretching the collar tight like a loofah
to rub that itch you couldn't get at
in the middle of your back.

I took it with your other things:
the shoes, shirts, blazer with brass buttons,
all since discarded, unworn.

For months it smelled of talc
or engine oil or maybe the sea –
of you anyway.

It's musty now, the colours fading,
the posture too slack for you
('Keep those shoulders straight!'),

nothing in the pockets but fluff.
I should take it to the dump
but first I try it on,

feeling it settle round me
like a skin I've slipped inside,
and when I look

there's you in the mirror,
serious, head tilted, sizing things up:
 'A perfect fit.'

Shirt

And afterwards she wants to wear your shirt –
for the smell of you recorded in the cotton,
or because what's yours is hers now.

She struts about, pretending to be you
or showing how stylish you look when a pretty girl
is modelling you. 'Does it suit me?' she asks,

climbing back into bed and kissing you, still with the shirt on,
which is disconcerting, like kissing yourself,
except that the shirt has grown breasts and the sleeves meet

behind your back, and in the mirror two people are fighting
to wear one shirt – impossible, when both are horizontal,
and yet somehow, between you, you fit.

Narcissus

Thinking the boiler had packed up from lack of oil
I climbed the rusty tank to peer down the hatch
and there I was, bright-faced and young again,
in the viscous black pool at the bottom.

Life Writing

You're trying to bring to life what's in your head,
a story that's discomfiting but true.
Your interest in inventing stuff's long dead.

You know that all worth saying's all been said
but strive to tell it straight and make it new.
You want to bring to life what's in your head.

The names of all the ones you took to bed,
the triumphs and disasters you lived through:
you'd like to set this down before you're dead.

You comb your troubled past from A to Z.
You drag forgotten memories into view.
Your memoir brings to life what's in your head.

But Tim, best mate at school, was really Ted,
and Tania's nut-brown eyes were turquoise-blue.
They phone you late at night and wish you dead.

The humour and affection go unread.
Your candour earns you merciless reviews.
Don't try to bring to life what's in your head.
It's safer telling lies about the dead.

Harvest

The combine comes to take the wheat.
The swallows steal the summer heat.
The mile-long sheets of soft grey mist
are fast to fall and slow to lift.

'All seasons pass': that's common lore.
And '*que sera*' and 'life moves on'.
But I'm not made to bear the loss
of soft brown flesh and sun-warmed stone.

And I can't face what's up ahead,
the shredded flowers, the hollow bed,
the pears wasp-eaten to the core.

A chilling pool, toy boats adrift,
a shrivelled windfall skimmed with frost.
Brief heat. Then death. That is the law.

Empties

Before the rain sets in
on the last day of August
I take the empties to the dump –
gin, vodka, wine, Pimms –

and stuff them in the mouth
of the bottle bank, which gapes
in mock surprise at so much
having been got through so fast,

mock because it knows by now
how our summers are passed
and the glasses are refilled
with friends round a wooden table

while the swallows dip
and the wheat ripens
and none of us thinking
that today will come,

with the bottles empty
and wasps circling like sharks
as the glass smashes
in the dark of the metal bin.

November

The low-slung sun.
The clocks turned back.
The honey fungus
on the firewood stack.

The pear's shrunk head,
gold skin gone black.
The spider in its rigging
like a steeplejack.

The Walk

I'll not forget our last walk together,
through the woods and down to the river,
which idled under a fogbank of midges,
too sleepy or sunstruck to stir.

At the second stile I held my hand out
as you leapt and refused to give yours back
till we'd passed through the field with the thistles
and the cowpats big as plates of Irish stew.

I can't remember what we talked about –
our work, probably, or children, or books,
not what we'd felt for each other, and still did.

But I'll not forget the walk, and your free hand
brushing the willows, and the water
sliding slowly as a funeral train.

Latecomer

All I'm saying has been said before, but not by me.
To ourselves we're always new, like the sun coming up
unaware it did so yesterday. The past might put us straight
but the past lives over the mountain, in a quiet meadow,
with horses grazing – horses we would recognise
if the stains on their flanks weren't hidden by trees.
Does the white mean they're getting old? Or is it the froth
from sweating saddles? We keep jostling for a better view
but can't get any closer than the quarry edge.
And really that's a kindness, like fog filling the valley
or the man with the megaphone suddenly noticing
the crowds have left and there's no one to tell
that the track and field events are over for the day
and that all previous records will stand.

Notes

'The Ballad of Shingle Street' – The setting is loosely based on the eponymous Suffolk village. In *The Rings of Saturn*, W. G. Sebald describes it as 'The most abandoned spot in the entire region… which now consists of just one wretched row of humble houses and cottages, and where I have never encountered a single human being', a view countered by Tim Miller (who lives there) in an affectionate essay in the *New Aldeburgh Anthology* (2009), compiled by Ariane Bankes and Jonathan Reekie.

In 1940 an attempted Nazi invasion, thwarted by a wall of fire and resulting in the deaths of hundreds of Germans, was rumoured to have taken place there. Though a couple of eyewitness accounts support the idea, it's likely the rumour was started deliberately to boost home morale; the wartime Underground Propaganda Committee (UPC) generated a number of similar whispering campaigns (code-named 'Sibs') about U-boat losses and ingenious Allied defence methods. The proximity of Orford Ness, where weapons experiments were carried out in the first half of the twentieth century, may have helped to popularise the myth. James Hayward's book *The Bodies on the Beach: Sealion, Shingle Street and the Burning Sea Myth of 1940* (2001), persuasively dispels it, while admitting that an air of mystery still surrounds the area.

Less in doubt is the extent of coastal erosion in East Anglia today.

'It Was Good While It Lasted' – These words were inscribed as the epitaph on Jimmy Savile's gravestone.

'Redacted' – The poem draws on Margaret Evison's book *Death of a Soldier: A Mother's Story* (2012), which recounts her efforts to establish the circumstances surrounding the death of her son Mark in Afghanistan in May 2009. A BBC3 documentary, *Our War*, contains harrowing footage, taken from head-cameras, of his colleagues' desperate struggle to save him.

'The Road to Wales' – The form was suggested to me by Peter Kahn, who is compiling an anthology called *The Golden Shovel*. It means taking a memorable phrase from a famous poem and using the words at the end of each line, so that the borrowed extract is laid out vertically on the right-hand margin of the created poem.

Acknowledgements

I am grateful to the editors of the following publications, where some of these poems first appeared: *Guardian, New Statesman, Poem, Standpoint, The Reader* and *Times Literary Supplement.*

All but one of the poems in 'THIS POEM...' are taken from a set of twenty-seven, first published in a pamphlet of the same name by smith|doorstop (2013). The exception is 'Redacted', which appeared in Carol Ann Duffy's anthology *1914: Poetry Remembers* (2013).